YOUR KNOWLEDGE HAS VALUE

- We will publish your bachelor's and master's thesis, essays and papers

- Your own eBook and book - sold worldwide in all relevant shops

- Earn money with each sale

Upload your text at www.GRIN.com and publish for free

Bibliographic information published by the German National Library:

The German National Library lists this publication in the National Bibliography; detailed bibliographic data are available on the Internet at http://dnb.dnb.de .

Imprint:

Copyright © 2014 GRIN Verlag, Open Publishing GmbH
Print and binding: Books on Demand GmbH, Norderstedt Germany
ISBN: 978-3-668-04822-5

This book at GRIN:

http://www.grin.com/en/e-book/305597/international-currencies-past-present-and-future

Evgeny Nosenko

International Currencies. Past, Present, and Future

GRIN Publishing

GRIN - Your knowledge has value

Since its foundation in 1998, GRIN has specialized in publishing academic texts by students, college teachers and other academics as e-book and printed book. The website www.grin.com is an ideal platform for presenting term papers, final papers, scientific essays, dissertations and specialist books.

Visit us on the internet:

http://www.grin.com/

http://www.facebook.com/grincom

http://www.twitter.com/grin_com

International Currencies

International Financial Markets
Higher School of Economics

Evgeny Nosenko

Contents

- "In our modern myopia, we usually forget that a world of separate national monies was not the primeval economic garden from which we evolved." (Zevin 1992, 46)

Carlo Cipolla has noted that monetary sovereignty is actually a very recent thing. "As late as the nineteenth century no western state enjoyed a complete monetary sovereignty.... In previous centuries ... the basic tenet of monetary organization [was] that foreign coins had the same rights as national coins and that they could freely come in and freely circulate without any particular limitation" (1967, 14). Essentially we have been living in the world of international currencies since 5th century B.C. and also have had currency competition in ones territory throughout the Middle ages, until around 19th century, when national states created sole legal tender laws for asserting power over creation and management of money for policy reasons, thus limiting foreign currency competition in its territory.

```
┌─────────────────────────────────────────────────────────────────┐
│                  History of International Currencies              │
│                                                                   │
│                                                                   │
│   The first genuinely international currency                      │
│   •   silver drachma of Athens (5th century B.C.E)                │
│                                                                   │
│   The "dollar of the Middle Ages"                                 │
│   •   Byzantine gold solidus (4th century)                        │
│                                                                   │
│   New generation of international currencies                      │
│   •   golden florin of Florence (1252)                            │
│   •   golden ducat (1284)                                         │
│                                                                   │
│                                                                   │
│                                                                   │
└─────────────────────────────────────────────────────────────────┘
```

The first international currency, the silver drachma of Athens, established itself around 5th century B.C.E. According to Benjamin Cohen (1998, 29) it circulated widely and was imitated long after the influence of Athens itself had faded and the Roman Empire came present. The reason was that the denarius was frequently debased and thus considered suspect, while the drachma (Groseclose 1976, 21), by the purity of its standard, kept alive the institutions of commerce and was also used in trade with India.

After the fall of the Roman Empire Byzantine gold solidus became the premier international currency. Dubbed as the "dollar of the Middle Ages" by Robert Lopez (1951). It circulated from Sri Lanka to the Baltic (Groseclose 1976, 49) and according to one 6th century monk "…is accepted anywhere from end to end of the earth. It is admired by all men and in all kingdoms, because no kingdom has a currency that can be compared to it" (Lopez 1951, 209; Cipolla 1967, 16).

The Renaissance ushered in a new era of international currencies. Golden florin of Florence, first issued in 1252, was dominant for nearly a century, until the great European crisis triggered by the Black Death of the 1340s (Cipolla 1989) and was then overtaken by the golden ducat of Venice in international exchange.

After the colonization of the New World, the Spanish-Mexican silver peso arose to dominance as nearly all additions to the world's silver supplies came from Spanish America, particularly from Mexico. Pesos circulated widely throughout not only the Western Hemisphere but, by way of the Philippines and Goa, much of the Far East as well. For the English colonists of North America, they were almost the only coin in use and served as an explicit model for the U.S. Congress when creating US dollars (Cohen 1998, 31). Even as late as 1830, pesos accounted for some 22 percent of the value of all coins in use in the United States (Rolnik and Weber 1986, 187).

Maria Theresa thaler is an example of not conventional international currency. It is a trade coin – money only created to pay for imports and not intended for domestic use. Although being quite unusual, it attained broad circulation and could be found in circulation in parts of Africa and the Arab world until the beginning of 20th century (Pond 1941).

Dominant in the 19th century was Britain's pound sterling, which owes its importance to path dependence. Benjamin Cohen (1998, 31):

> With the end of the Napoleonic Wars in 1815, foreigners increasingly found themselves earning large incomes in Britain or in countries making payments to Britain; or alternatively making payments to Britain or to countries earning incomes there. It was only natural that commercial debts would come to be cleared through London and denominated in sterling; and as London's capital exports grew, eventually to overshadow all other financial centers, network

externalities made the pound more appealing as a longer-term store of value as well. Especially after 1860, even as much of the developed world moved toward consolidation of a global gold standard, sterling gained acceptance nearly everywhere for both transactions and investment purposes.

As A.C.L Day notes (1954, 16), it is a case of network externalities, strength of sterling attracted more strength and more importance, a fact also aided by colonial expansion of the British Empire.

During 1850s US started minting its own currency – dollar. A lot of different currencies circulated in US until 1861, but then the dollar became the country's sole legal tender, later standardized with the creation of the FED in 20th century (Cohen 1998, 34). The reasons why dollar overtook sterling lay mostly in the world-wars period of 20th century, when US was a creditor to Britain and others, accumulating gold reserves in the process and besides US was left relatively untouched from war casualties, helping them to maintain and grow their production capabilities.

Types and Useage

- Currency types by FX rate regimes
- Exchange arrangement with no separate legal tender
- Currency board arrangement
- Conventional pegged arrangement
- Pegged exchange rate within horizontal bands
- Crawling peg
- Crawling band
- Managed floating with no pre-announced path for the exchange rate
- Independently floating

Types and Useage

Currency Distribution in Foreign Exchange Transactions

Currency	2001	2004	2007	2011
US dollar	89.9	88	85.6	84.9
euro	37.9	37.4	37	39.1
Japanese yen	23.5	20.8	17.2	19
Pound sterling	13	16.5	14.9	12.9
Australian dollar	4.3	6	6.6	7.6
Swiss franc	6	6	6.8	6.4
Other currencies	25.4	25.3	31.9	30.1

Source: Bank of International Settlement (BIS), Triennial Bank Survey, 2010

Types and Useage

- Mediums of Exchange
  - Foreign exchange trading, trade settlement
  - Interventions

- Store of value
  - Investments
  - Reserves

- Unit of account
  - Trade invoicing
  - Anchor currency

```
┌─────────────────────────────────────────────────────────────┐
│                                                               │
│          Costs and Benefits of International Currencies       │
│                                                               │
│    •  Benefits for the issuer:                                │
│          –  Lowering transaction costs                        │
│          –  Seigniorage                                       │
│          –  Macroeconomic flexibility                         │
│          –  Leverage                                          │
│          –  Enhancing reputation                              │
│                                                               │
│    •  Disadvantages for the issuer:                           │
│          –  Appreciation of the currency                      │
│          –  Macroeconomic vulnerability                       │
│          –  Policy responsibility                             │
│                                                               │
│                                                               │
│                                                               │
└─────────────────────────────────────────────────────────────┘
```

There are a number of benefits for countries – issuers of international currencies. First of all, *lowering transaction costs* boosts profits in the banking sector because it becomes easier for companies and banks to create liabilities abroad; moreover, there may be additional bank commissions charged for an increased volume of transactions. What is more, businesses can expand abroad and operate in their home currency, thus lowering exchange risk. Secondly, issuance of international money gives countries an advantage of *seigniorage* from foreign accumulations of cash (given the fact that cash represents 0-interest loan to the issuing country) and from foreign accumulation of financial claims. Another advantage is *macroeconomic flexibility:* the country has the ability to finance its payments deficits with its own money, so it can easier achieve public spending objectives. One possible advantage for issuers of international currencies is *leverage* in the meaning of influence on other countries through control of access to financial resources. (Cohen, 2012, pp. 14-16). As Chey demonstrates (Chey 2012, p. 66), *enhancing reputation* may be considered another overall use of a currency can promote the issuer's reputation (soft power).

Otherwise, there are risks associated with issuance of an international currency. Firstly, increased foreign demand can cause exchange rate *appreciation*, what can worsen the position of exporters of goods and services. Secondly, risks of volatile movements of the international currency make the money demand less stable (*macroeconomic vulnerability*); therefore it may be more difficult to target inflation and growth rates. Then, there is an increased *policy responsibility:* responsibility for global operations (monetary policy have to be modified when the crisis arises). (Cohen, 2012, pp. 16-18)

Currency internalization involves a *variety of roles* (different functions, e.g. medium of exchange, at different levels – public or official). As international currency has different roles, the positive and negative impact of these roles has to be separately assessed and measured at all levels.

```
┌─────────────────────────────────────────────────────────────────────┐
│                        Alternative Currencies                         │
│                                                                       │
│                                                                       │
│      •  LETSystems                                                    │
│      •  Liberty dollar, Brixton pound                                 │
│      •  Valcambi Combibar                                             │
│                                                                       │
│      •  Bitcoin                                                       │
│      •  Peer-to-peer electronic cash system                           │
│      •  "Mining"                                                      │
│      Pros                                                             │
│      •  No possiblilty (yet) of governmental interference             │
│      •  Untraceable                                                   │
│      Cons                                                             │
│      •  Subject to scams                                              │
│      •  Volatility                                                    │
│                                                                       │
│                                                                       │
└─────────────────────────────────────────────────────────────────────┘
```

LETSystems, Liberty dollar, Brixton pound and Valcambi Combibar are examples of alternative currencies, but they are mostly community based and/or with small significance. Truly international alternative currency is Bitcoin. Created by Satoshi Nakamoto in 2009, it is a peer-to-peer electronic cash system, using which its users can buy goods from merchants, who accept Bitcoins or make trades within themselves. Central theme in Bitcoin is mining, meaning creation of Bitcoins via running complicated mathematical equations on ones computer, through which blocks are created and one receives prize - Bitcoins. It is also possible to obtain Bitcoins by buying them from Bitcoin exchange for US dollars.

Bitcoin has limited supply, so it is not possible for 3rd parties to intervene and create inflation. Also because of the cryptic nature of Bitcoin, it is impossible to trace, making it safe haven for privacy and security enthusiasts.

There have been incidents people losing all their money because of wallets being hacked. Recently Bitcoin price has been subject to some volatility, more on that on slide 12.

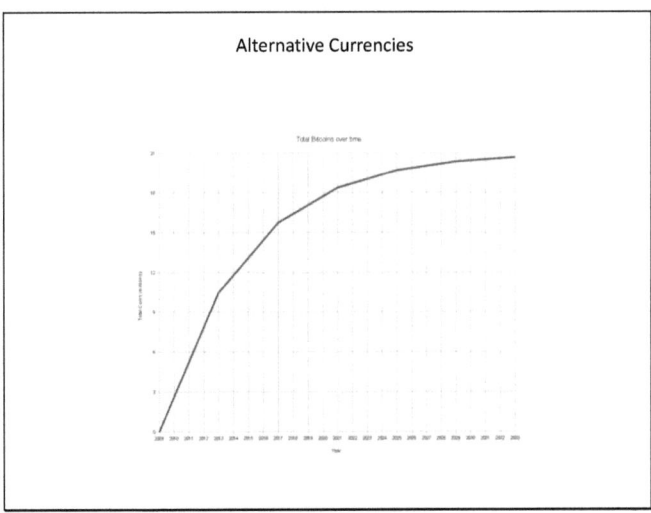

Alternative Currencies

Source: Wikipedia, https://en.bitcoin.it/wiki/Controlled_supply

Graphic illustrates the total supply of 21 million Bitcoins, reaching its limit in 2033. Also shows the decrease of Bitcoin creation rate, which halves in every 4 years. For years 2009-2013 the prize for creating 210000 blocks is 50 Bitcoins per block, for next period of 210000 blocks it is 25 Bitcoins per block and so on.

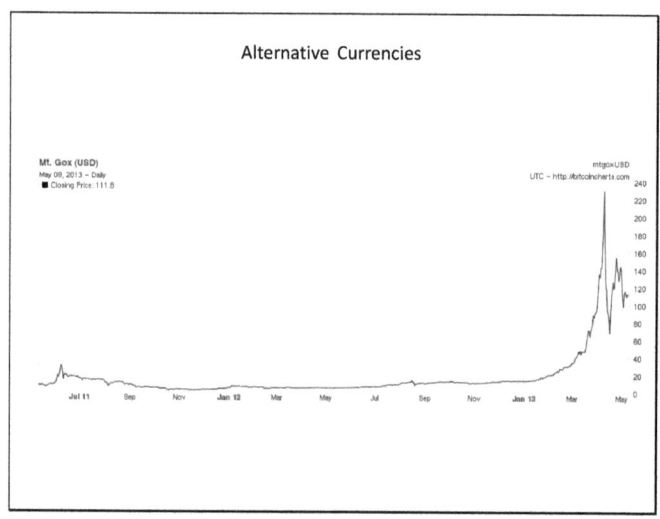

Source: http://bitcoincharts.com/charts/mtgoxUSD#rg730ztgCzm1g10zm2g25

It shows the closing prices of dollars per Bitcoin in Bitcoin exchange market Mt. Gox, for period July 2011 to May 09, 2013. Graphic indicates fairly stable base and the speculative bubble of Bitcoin in March – May 2013.

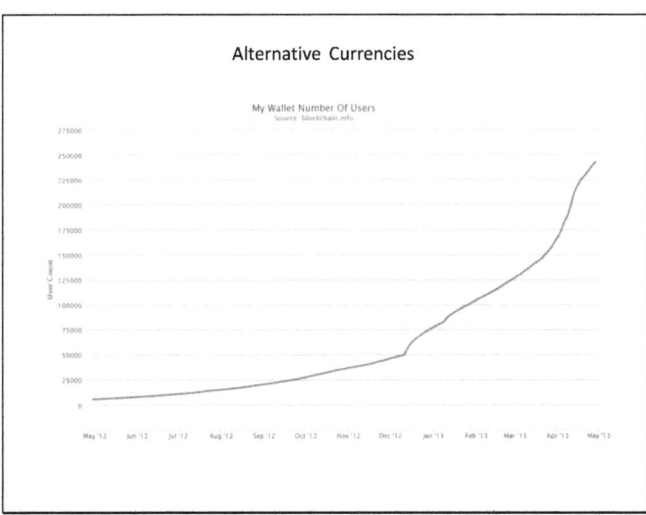

Source: http://blockchain.info/charts/my-wallet-n-users

The cryptic nature of Bitcoin makes it impossible to accurately know the amount of its users. One broad estimate is that it is somewhere between 10000 and 1000000 unique users. This graphic aims to give insight into it by showing the amount of wallets (user = wallet) in My Wallet service, although one physical user (person) can have more than one wallet.

```
┌─────────────────────────────────────────────────────────────────────┐
│                                                                       │
│                  Future of International Currencies                   │
│                                                                       │
│                                                                       │
│     •  Current position of the dollar                                 │
│                                                                       │
│     •  Strengths                                                      │
│          − Most important international currency                      │
│          − Inertia effects                                            │
│          − Shifting away from the dollar implies currency converting costs │
│          − FX markets: Network externalities and economy of scale     │
│          − The USA is the supreme political and military power        │
│                                                                       │
│     •  Weaknesses                                                     │
│          − Large current account deficit and foreign debt             │
│          − Loose fiscal and monetary policies                         │
│          − Rise of China as a geopolitical rival of the USA           │
│                                                                       │
│                                                                       │
└─────────────────────────────────────────────────────────────────────┘
```

Given the fact that the US dollar remains the dominant international currency, the prospects for the international financial order largely depend on the dollar's future position. This chapter is concerned with the issue of the contemporary status of the dollar, the euro and the yuan as international currencies and the future changes in their international position.

The available evidence seems to suggest that the position of the dollar as an international currency is still relatively unchanged. A major part of international trade and credit transactions is executed in the dollar, a relatively big part of currency reserves of central banks is held in the US dollars (Belke 2011, p. 4). Inertia effects in using the dollar as a global currency because of habitual use and institutional rigidity play in favour of the dollar's future use. Many countries do not shift away from the dollar because of high would-be costs of currency converting. Economies of scale and network externalities give the dollar an advantage in international financial markets (Wilson et al. 2012, p.3). Further evidence supporting the position of the dollar is the solid political base of the USA: from the view of international political economy, the country is one of the political and military powers in the world, therefore the dollar's economic attributes as an international currency remain strong (Chey 2012, p. 61).

In contrast, the huge current account deficit and foreign debt of the US are likely to undermine the global confidence in the dollar (Eichengreen 2005, p. 17). Loose US fiscal and monetary policies may reduce the willingness to use the dollar for transactions and as a reserve currency. Moreover, the rise of China as a geopolitical rival of the US and seems to worsen the position of the dollar (Chey 2012, p. 62).

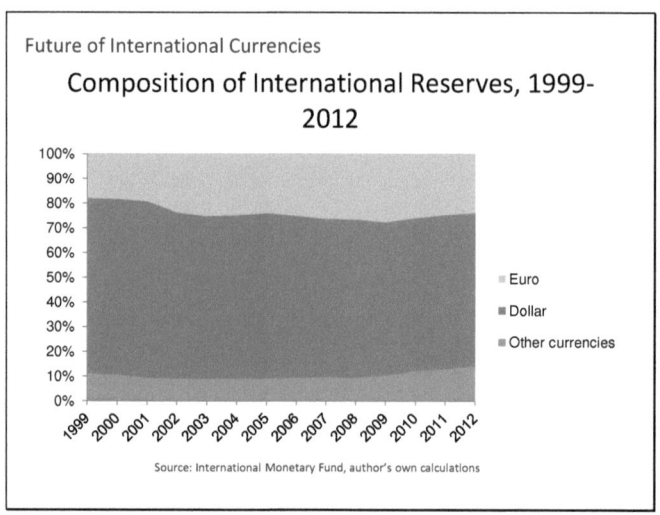

Source: International Monetary Fund. Electronic resource: http://www.imf.org; author's own calculations.

The graph demonstrates the composition of international reserves in 1999-2012. The euro's share rose from 18% in 1999 to 27% in 2012, while the share of the dollar in international reserves shrank by approximately 10% during this period. The share of other currencies rose slightly up to 12% in 2012.

```
┌─────────────────────────────────────────────────────────────────┐
│                    Future of International Currencies             │
│                                                                   │
│   •  Current position of the euro                                 │
│                                                                   │
│   •  Strengths                                                    │
│        −  The rise of the global share of the euro in international reserves │
│        −  Relative sizes of economies and financial markets of the US and │
│           Europe                                                  │
│        −  European trade partners shift to the euro               │
│                                                                   │
│                                                                   │
│   •  Weaknesses                                                   │
│        −  Fragile political base                                  │
│        −  Lack of supranational regulator                         │
│        −  Lower liquidity of the bond market than in the US       │
│        −  Regional character of the euro as an international currency │
│                                                                   │
│                                                                   │
└─────────────────────────────────────────────────────────────────┘
```

The emergence of the euro as a new global currency in 1999 fostered the debate on the dollar's future role, and nowadays the euro is the only challenger to overrun the dollar for the key international currency position. The global share of international reserves in the euro rose from 18% in 1999 to 27% in 2012 (Belke 2011, p. 4). The European and the US economies and financial markets have relative sizes; countries in Eastern Europe and Asia have shifted to European markets according to their international trade patterns (Chey 2012, p. 62). These facts provide confirmatory evidence that the euro gains confidence as an international currency.

Otherwise, a weaker political base for the euro and absence of supranational regulator damage the position of the currency (Wilson et al. 2012, p.3). Moreover, the European bond market suffers the lack of liquidity and size in comparison to the market of the US Treasury bills, mostly due to the heterogeneity of the countries comprising the monetary union (Wilson et al. 2012, p. 6). The euro's international role has nowadays only regional character. (Chey 2012, p. 62).

```
┌─────────────────────────────────────────────────────────────┐
│                Future of International Currencies             │
│                                                               │
│   •  Current position of the yuan                             │
│                                                               │
│   •  Strengths                                                │
│        −  Large size of the Chinese economy                   │
│        −  Optimistic macroeconomic indicators                 │
│        −  International political economy: the rise of China   │
│           as an economic and military power                   │
│                                                               │
│   •  Weaknesses                                               │
│        −  Underdevelopment of capital markets                 │
│        −  Low convertibility of the currency                  │
│        −  Authoritarian nature of the political regime         │
│                                                               │
│                                                               │
└─────────────────────────────────────────────────────────────┘
```

There has been an inconclusive debate about whether the yuan can become a new widely used international currency. Large size of the economy and attractive macroeconomic indicators, such as strong economic growth, low inflation rates and current account surplus, are the main factors that can have a positive impact on the yuan's future use as an international currency (Chey 2012, p. 62). Meanwhile, underdevelopment of the capital market along with the authoritarian political regime lower the confidence in the yuan.

The question about the future of the international currency system causes much debate nowadays. On the ground of the aforesaid evidence we can argue that despite of the facts against the use of the dollar as an international currency, nowadays it plays a central role in international trade and finance. The future of the international financial system depends on the dollar's position.

There seems to be no compelling reason to argue that the fact that the reserve currency country is running current account deficit and has a large foreign debt may worsen its position as a banker to the world. Eichengreen argues that if the foreign debt of the US keeps growing, creditors will be not willing to hold more of it, what can lead to the currency depreciation and a higher inflation in the US. It will have negative impact on output and economic growth, leading to even a sharper drop of the dollar and making foreign central banks to shift out from the dollar to avoid losses (Eichengreen 2005, p. 20). In this case the euro will gain more importance than it enjoys today, but it is unlikely to overcome the dollar at the global scale because of a strong regional character of the currency.

In a more positive scenario, given the political conditions and confidence in the dollar's stability, the currency will preserve the role of the dominant one in the world losing partly its importance due to the inevitable diversification in the international financial market. As Gaspar shows, international investors and central banks will diversify their portfolios to lower their macroeconomic risks (Gaspar 2004, p. 3). The future of the euro will depend mostly on China, because, as Chey emphasizes, China will transfer a part of its reserves on the euro that will cause a global shift to the euro of other countries (Chey 2012, p. 63).

In both cases the yuan does not seem to become a new challenger for a dominant international currency role unless the Chinese authorities will develop Chinese financial markets, what would require reforming of the country's model of growth.

The consensus view seems to be that in long run the international currency pattern will be represented by two or three currencies (the dollar, the euro and probably the yuan). The US dollar is going to lose its dominance due to a worse position of the US economy, but its problems are not large to cause an immediate shift to another currency. The euro is likely gain importance because of inevitable diversification in international financial markets.

Many researchers demonstrate that the current international currency system requires to be reformed. Salvatore argues that it is characterized by a wide variety of exchange rates agreements with high exchange rate volatility, negatively impacting international competitiveness and international trade (Salvatore 2011, pp. 779-782).

Mundell proposed a radical reforming of the current international currency system by in fact creating a single world currency. The USA, Europe and Japan (AEJ) represent 60% of the world GDP, so the international monetary system is dominated by these economies. The best way for small countries is fixing exchange rates to one of the AEJ currencies as an alternative to inflation or monetary targeting. They will import the inflation of a large country, and the balance of payments will be kept in equilibrium by changes in the money supply through changes in reserves. The AEJ counties have similar inflation rates, so they may fix their exchange rates or issue the same currency. If the AEJ countries had the same currency, the other countries would inevitably join the currency union by fixing their exchange rates, therefore creating the common world currency. The world central bank would maintain price stability in the monetary union. (Mundell 2000, pp. 281-289).

The implementation of these reforms does not seem practicable, because, as Salvatore argues, there is a lack of coordination of macroeconomic policies among the leading countries, implying different inflation-unemployment tradeoffs (Salvatore 2011, p. 783).

References

Belke, A. et al. 2011. The Future of the International Monetary System. *DIW Economic Bulletin*, Vol. 4. Pp. 11-17.

Cipolla, Carlo M. (1967). Money, Prices, and Civilization in the Mediterranean World: Fifth to Seventeenth Century. New York: Gordian Press.

Cipolla, Carlo M. (1989). Money in Seventeenth Century Florence. Berkeley: University of California Press.

Chey, H.-K. (2012). Theories of International Currencies and the Future of the World Monetary Order. *International Studies Review,* Vol. 14, pp. 51-77.

Cohen, B. J. 1998. The Geography of Money. Ithaca: Cornell University Press.

Cohen, B.J. 2012. 'The Benefits and Costs of an International Currency: Getting the Calculus Right', *Open Econ Rev,* Vol. 23, pp. 13–31

Day, A. C. L. 1954. The Future of Sterling. Clarendon Press

Eichengreen, B. 2005. 'Sterling's Past, Dollar's Future: Historical Perspectives on Reserve Currency Competition.,' *NBER WORKING PAPER SERIES.*

Groseclose, Elgin (1976). Money and Man: A Survey of Monetary Experience, 4th ed. Norman: University of Oklahoma Press.

Lopez, Robert S. (1951). "The Dollar of the Middle Ages." Journal of Economic History 11, no. 3 (Summer): 209-34.

Mundell, R. 2000. '*Currency Areas, Volatility and Intervention',* Journal of Policy Modeling, Vol. 22(3), pp. 281–299

Pond, Shepard. 1941. "The Maria Theresa Thaler: A Famous Trade Coin." Bulletin of the Business History Society 15, no. 2 (April): 26-31.

Rolnick, Arthur J & Weber, Warren E, 1986. "Gresham's Law or Gresham's Fallacy?," Journal of Political Economy, University of Chicago Press, vol. 94(1), pages 185-99, February.

Salvatore, D. 2011.'The future tri-polar international monetary system', *Journal of Policy Modeling*, Vol. 33, Issue 5, pp. 776-785

Wilson, H. et al, 2012. Is the Dollar the Uncontended Champion as the International Reserve Currency or Does the Euro Stand a Chance? *International Journal Of Business Research.* Vol. 12, pp.146-153.

Zevin, Robert. 1992. "Are World Financial Markets More Open? If So, Why and with What Effects?" In Tariq Banuri and Juliet B. Schor, eds., Financial Openness and National Autonomy. Oxford: Clarendon Press.